SELLING SKILLS

SELF-STUDY SERIES

SC SHORE
CONSULTING

ABOUT THE AUTHOR

Jeff Shore is a highly sought-after sales keynote speaker, author and consultant. For more than three decades, Jeff has guided sales executives and sales teams in large and small companies across the globe to deliver profitable customer-first sales results.

In a crowded field of sales keynote speakers and sales training programs, Jeff Shore stands out with his research-based "buying formula" methodology. Combining his extensive front-line sales experience with the latest leading-edge research into buyer psychology, Jeff has created a highly effective, personalized way to reset sales paradigms and deliver industry-leading results.

Jeff holds the prestigious Certified Speaking Professional designation from the National Speakers Association (NSA) and is a member of the NSA's exclusive Million Dollar Speakers' Group. Jeff tailors every keynote to your business and your team while electrifying your audience through captivating real-world case studies, inspiring personal stories, hard-working and straightforward sales strategies, and his engaging trademark humor.

Jeff won't just teach you how to sell…he'll show you how to change your mindset AND how to change your world.

jeffshore.com
jeff@jeffshore.com
(844) 54-SHORE

Dealing with Challenging Customers In Sales

7 Reality-Based Techniques for Tackling Tough Customers

BY JEFF SHORE

ISBN: 978-0-9884915-5-7

Cover and page design by Kista Cook

Shore Consulting books are available at special quantity discounts to use as premiums and sales promotions or for use in corporate training programs. To contact a representative, please visit the Contact page at www.jeffshore.com or call +1 844-54-SHORE.

CONTENTS

PREFACE

We've all had them. They are inevitable in the world of sales. They come in various forms and styles, but come they will. And how we deal with them will directly determine our level of sales success.

Who are they? They are the "Challenging Customers."

On the one hand, we all would love to have some kind of sales "kryptonite" to keep them at bay; I'm fairly confident that we won't be able to find such a mineral.

But I would contend that the strategy of top sales professionals should be to embrace challenging customers. The process of understanding and serving challenging customers is the key to unlocking the door to big-time sales success. While other salespeople are blowing off challenging prospects, top professionals are landing deals right and left.

To be certain, challenging customers will require more energy than most, but they also represent a market share that too many in our profession simply dismiss.

In this short book I identify seven types of difficult buyers and share insights into how you can guide each of them through a positive purchasing process. You'll discover that the problem is not typically related to the buyer's character as much as it is about their purchasing style.

Once you gain that mindset, you will expand your pool of potential purchasers and be on your way to establishing a distinct advantage over your competitors.

So, roll up your sleeves and let's get to work. Trust me… it will be worth it!

Jeff Shore

Dealing with Challenging Customers In Sales
The Mindset

INTRODUCTION

INTRODUCTION:

The Mindset

I was at a Courtyard by Marriott in Indianapolis. I had all kinds of flight problems and did not arrive at the hotel until just after midnight, frustrated and dog-tired.

I approached the front desk with a desire only to be horizontal—soon. "Shore, checking in. Here's my license and credit card."

The young lady at the counter smiled politely and responded, "I'm sorry, sir. We are sold out this evening."

Already grumpy, but now becoming aware that they had oversold the hotel and given away my room, I was quickly into the first stages of an oncoming fury. Still, I held it together.

"No, I have a reservation. Find me a room."

"I'm sorry, sir, but every room in the hotel is full. We don't seem to have a reservation for you."

Enough. It is on. No more Mr. Nice Guy.

"Look, I made a reservation and I held it with my credit card. If I had not shown up, you would have charged me for the night. Don't tell me you don't have a room. You do have a room that you gave away to someone else. So I want you to walk down the hall, knock on the door, tell them you've made a mistake, and give me the room that I reserved."

At this point, I think I qualified for the moniker "challenging customer."

Question: Did I have a right to be upset? It was past midnight, I had made a reservation, and I had no place to sleep.

Let's get back to the story.

"Sir, you said you made a reservation yourself. Do you have any documentation for that?"

Aha! The smoking gun! I did, in fact, have a copy of the reservation. I handed it over to her with a smug "I've got you now" look on my face.

She spent a few moments looking at the paper and typing into her computer before saying, "Mr. Shore, I see what happened. It's a common mistake. You made a reservation for tomorrow night. And yes, you are in our system for tomorrow evening."

(insert comic sound effect of your choice here)

Go back and look at the question I posed a moment ago. I asked you if I had a right to be upset. Based on what you knew of the story at the time you probably said that I did.

To the profound credit of the front desk employee (and to the Courtyard Marriott as a whole, for that matter), she went on to say, "I'm so sorry. I have a list of other hotels in the area. Let me make some calls and see if we can find you a room."

What? She had every reason to match me, snarky for snarky. She would be well within her rights to say, "Thank you so much for that boatload of attitude thrown my way in the middle of the night. Remember the door where you came in? That door, surprisingly, leads you out. That is, if you're bright enough to get that part right. Good night now."

Walking a Mile

Can we begin with a handful of honesty? We have all—every one of us at some point in our past—worn the moniker of "challenging customer." Whether it was ultimately warranted or not, we have walked in those shoes.

Note that in those moments we would have justified our belligerence as being completely appropriate. I certainly did at that hotel in Indianapolis.

That is a very important point; don't miss it. From our own perspective our behavior is neither belligerent or inappropriate. We always feel justified to act in the manner we choose.

Put it this way: There is no such thing as irrational behavior. Every outburst, every comment, every sneer—all are rational actions in that moment. That is true for each of us, and it is true for our customers.

Because of this truth it would stand to reason that the most appropriate action on our part would be neither judgment nor derision, but rather a desire to truly understand.

The Battle Within

You might be saying that some customers walk through the door with a chip on the shoulder, and I would agree. But where did that chip come from? Is that just who they are? Do they treat their friends and family members the same way they treat an unfamiliar salesperson? I would contend that they do not.

Tim is a friend of mine who could best be described as financially conservative in his dealings. Accordingly, he never purchases new cars, preferring to buy only late model used cars.

Tim confesses that he approaches used car dealerships with fear and trepidation. In fact, he admits that his attitude is far less than kind when he talks to a salesperson. His defenses are high and his trust is low. His demeanor makes that obvious.

Question: Does that make Tim a bad person? A mean person? A snarky person?

None of the above. It makes him a used car buyer. But in Tim's case it means that he has direct experience in dealing with a less-than-honest dealer in his past. He knows deep down that not all used car salespeople and dealerships are dishonest, but having been taken advantage of once he is defensive and combative from the get-go.

Again, there is no such thing as irrational behavior. In his own mind, Tim is perfectly justified in being less than his best self in this situation.

What might have happened to your customer before he walked through the door? What were his experiences? What stories had he heard? What preconceptions had already been formed?

Now layer on top of that the enormous fear that goes along with making a large financial decision. The fear of a bad choice. The fear of commitment. The fear of change. The fear of being taken advantage of.

Doesn't it stand to reason that often you will meet customers whose behavior is less than pleasant?

Behavior? Or Character?

In light of that perspective, what is the number one crime committed daily by sales professionals everywhere?

The greatest crime is to confuse behavior with character. To define the individual as being mean versus *acting* mean. There is a ginormous difference. When we find ourselves in stressful situations we simultaneously find an adjustment to our behavior.

Many years ago my best friend from childhood was killed in a plane crash. I was devastated. And if you met me for the first time in those days immediately after the accident you would have likely described me as being cold, aloof, or downright mean.

Would those descriptions have been accurate? Only if you were describing my behaviors, but in no way describing my character.

In other words, there is such a thing as *situationally* difficult customers. This does not make them evil people. Your customers are good and decent people despite their behaviors. They have real friends. They have real jobs. They go to real churches and eat at real restaurants, but put them in challenging circumstances and you are bound to see difficult behavior.

But wait. Are there exceptions? Are there some who really are downright mean?

Maybe. But what good is it to assume such a thing. As soon as you believe that some people are just plain jerks you give reason and justification for your own jerk-like response.

And if you can only find sales success when you are dealing with happy, pleasant, well-adjusted people, I have very bad news for you. Your success will be limited.

The Real Question: Who is in Control?

Perhaps it is time to toss this critical question in your direction: Who is in charge of your attitude?

We all know the easy answer. On the surface we agree that we are 100% responsible for our own attitude. In practice, in those times when we are getting nothing but grief from a challenging customer, that truth does not always hold up.

So what do the experts say? Here are two quotes that are definitely worth memorizing:

> *"No one can make you feel bad without your permission."*
> **– Eleanor Roosevelt**

> *"Everything can be taken from a man except for one thing—the last of the human freedoms—the ability to choose one's attitude in any given set of circumstances."*
> **– Viktor Frankl**

The wise sages of our time are in agreement. This is on us. We decide how we will respond to negative behavior. And decide we must. Our natural instinct will put us in a fighting stance. A hugging stance would be more appropriate.

Suppose a customer comes into your sales office with a 50-pound sack of negative energy. Suppose also that you are committed to being your best self. Intensely negative meets decidedly positive.

Mark my words; five minutes into the conversation someone will have changed. Either their negative energy turns positive or your energy turns sour.

On the other hand, if the customer comes in with negativity and you meet it with negativity, what happens? An explosion, that's what.

This is a game that you cannot afford to lose. The only way to win is with a firm commitment to your own positive approach. This is a choice, and that choice must be renewed day by day, hour by hour, customer by customer.

The Good News

Is there an upside? You bet there is.

You see, that negative customer will offend weaker salespeople all over town. They will blow him off and shut him down.

Ask the veterans in your industry and they will all tell you the same thing. When you can bring this guy around he will be your best friend and often your strongest source of referrals. If you can take the negative and turn it into a positive, the sky is truly the limit.

Outlast with your own positive energy and they will trust you more than any other salesperson. Why? Because you proved to be trustworthy. After all, if you crumbled at the first sign of a challenge you have failed the test.

Charlie Plum once said, "Adversity is a terrible thing to waste." True words when applied to the challenging customer.

The Challenge

Make it a challenge. A game, if you will. A game that you do not lose. Here are the rules of the game:

1. I determine my own attitude.
2. I make that determination before I meet the customer.
3. I vow to outlast the negative approach.
4. The worst-case scenario: a draw...but my attitude is still intact.
5. I will not bring negative emotion from one conversation into the next.

SELF-STUDY QUESTIONS:

1. *Think of a recent prospect you worked with who was a challenge for you. Were your interactions with them successful? What could you have done differently to make the interaction more pleasant for you and the customer?*

2. *Create your own mantra. What can you say or do every day to ensure you get your mindset right and bring your best self to every interaction with your prospects?*

3. *If you catch yourself being negative or defensive with a prospect, what could you do (or say) to reset the conversation and gain their trust?*

Dealing with Challenging Customers In Sales

Entitled Customers

CHAPTER 1:

Entitled Customers

In the pages that follow I will break down these challenging customers into seven different groups. Each group represents different behaviors or characteristics of challenging customers. Fair warning: If at any point you feel even the slightest bit of derision for the customers I describe, please—PLEASE—go back and reread the book's introduction. Your mindset is critical.

Let's start with the entitled customer.

My guess is you've heard this one: "I'm paying $*X,XXX* (thousands) for this product and I deserve to get it the way I want it!"

Now let me ask a question: Have you ever said that or felt the same way as a customer who has? I know I have.

There is something about spending a lot of money that tends to trigger a sense of "I want it the way I want it." The psychology behind that is fascinating. It comes down to a comparison of sacrifices.

The Sacrifice Syndrome

Suppose you are going to spend $40,000 to have a pool built in your backyard. You want it the way you want it and you are not overly concerned about whether you offend a salesperson in the process. If you feel somewhat entitled, so be it. It's your money.

But it's actually more than just your money. Think about it. How long did it take for you to earn that $40,000? How much of your life did you sacrifice in order to come up with that much money? Or how much will you give up (sacrifice) in the form of monthly payments going forward?

Now compare your sacrifice to that of your pool company. "I'm paying $40,000 for this pool. The least that company can do is throw in a waterfall."

In that scenario, the customer's *perception* is that his sacrifice—his pain, if you will—far exceeds that of the provider. The owner of the pool company is thinking, "This guy is nuts. I'm not going to give away a huge chunk of my profit just because he is pushy. I'm going to tell him that if he doesn't want to pay for my pool, he can just go jump in a lake." (See what I did there?)

The Battle of Perceptions

In any form of conflict there will always be two sides of the story. This certainly holds true with the prospects who seem to think you owe them something as soon as they walk through the door. They carry an attitude that suggests they can demand from you whatever their heart desires.

But is it possible that the sales professional has his or her own sense of entitlement? I'm talking about the sense that the customer owes us a good attitude and polite behavior.

The battle begins when *either side* believes that the other has violated our perception.

From your first impressions, you might be perceiving that this customer is acting in an entitled manner. Yet if you were to ask the customer if they believed they were acting in this way I guarantee you they would say, "No."

Getting Your Head Right

It is up to us to challenge our own perception with three questions:

1. "Am I seeking to understand?"
2. "Am I being fair?"
3. "Am I assessing this person's motives correctly?"

It is critical that we gain the proper mindset over the situation. We must understand that this entitlement mentality is not an issue of character. It is an issue of style.

I will admit that some people are more demanding than most. This is their style, their normal approach and buying method. It is what they have always known. Perhaps they had parents who behaved this way or maybe they grew up in a culture where it was natural to ask for everything.

To you, it may be off-putting. To them, it is normal.

Here's the problem. When someone does something that is off-putting to us, we tend to make a character judgment about that person. That's a big mistake. It is always best if we consider their behavior as a style issue and not a character issue. This allows us to more positively approach the sales conversation.

One other thing to consider: How do buyers know if they got everything they could out of a purchase transaction? They ask. And ask. And ask again.

The perspective in this case is that customers want to be assured that they got the best terms possible. That's noble, when you think about it. And the only way to know for sure is to press until the salesperson stops saying "yes" to their demands.

How to Handle the Entitled Buyer?

1. Show Demonstrable Respect

It is the duty and obligation of a sales professional to remain positive and respectful about the customer's approach. As soon as we see this as a war, the battle will already have been lost. We must visibly demonstrate our calm confidence regardless of the demands that the customer brings.

One of the ways you can show that calm confidence is to make sure you are smiling during the conversation—even when you are saying no. The smile conveys that you are not easily rattled and that you are confident in your responses. When you are practicing your responses, remember to do so with a smile on your face.

2. Establish Authority Early in the Conversation

Suppose a customer pushes for something outside your sales limitations. You might reply, "I totally respect your request, and I understand why that is important to you. Let me tell you why we will not grant your request."

Note the phrase, "we will not…" as opposed to, "we cannot…"

I use this definitive language very specifically. Many salespeople might say "We can't do that," but that tends to rub the entitled customer the wrong way. What they hear is, "We can do that; we just don't want to." They believe you can grant the request and will probably throw that back at you by saying "I think you can." All of a sudden, you are on the defensive and the sales conversation becomes much more difficult.

You are much better off getting ahead of the conversation by saying something like, "Let me explain why we won't do that" or "We won't be able to meet that request and here's our rationale." When you have a valid and logical reason for denying the request you have a much greater chance of appeasing this customer.

3. Give in on a Few Little Things

Often it does not take much to appease this entitled customer. Small victories can mean a lot. It conveys a message that says, "We are not unreasonable people. We understand your desire to have it the way you want it. While we will not grant you your initial request, I think we can offer you this instead."

Summary

This is a battle over who controls the emotional tone in the conversation. So stay strong. Stay positive. Explain that you respect where they are coming from, but—politely and firmly—make it clear there are limitations in the sales process.

Entitled buyers can be tough but they are still potential buyers. If you approach them the right way, you can lead them through the purchase process with positive results.

SELF-STUDY QUESTIONS:

1. *Think of a recent prospect or buyer you worked with that fits the characteristics of an "entitled customer." How did you handle your interactions with them? What would or could you have done differently to make the interactions with them more pleasant and productive for you and them?*

2. *What specific steps can you take to practice working on your responses to entitled customers?*

3. *How would you respond to a customer who says, "I can buy the same thing for less from (your competitor)"? Write out a script you can use to practice your response to the question.*

. . . .

. . . .

. . . .

. . . .

. . . .

. . . .

. . . .

Dealing with Challenging Customers In Sales

Mean Customers

CHAPTER 2

CHAPTER 2:

Mean Customers

I recently received an email from a sales professional which read as follows: *"Jeff – I used a technique that I read in one of your books. It backfired in my face. Robert."*

Intrigued, I responded with a simple request: "Tell me more about that."

He wrote back: *"I said to a customer—just as I had learned from your book—the following opening statement: 'So, you're out doing some shopping around. How is your search going? Are you having fun?' He responded, 'No, I'm not shopping. I'm just looking. And I don't need any of your slick sales talk!'"*

Ouch. Tough way to start a sales office conversation.

Question: What did this salesperson say that so totally and completely set that customer off? What heinous technique would have merited such a mean-spirited response?

Answer: It doesn't matter what the salesperson said. That response from the customer was pre-determined *before he got out of his car.* He had a burr in his saddle long before he walked through the door.

Challenging customers come in all shapes, sizes...and demeanors. In this chapter, we're going to look at dealing with the mean customer, that individual who comes through the door in an aggressive, confrontational, and perhaps condescending manner.

Rule #1: Do NOT Respond in Kind

It is no secret that when you meet someone who is showing you a snarky, nasty demeanor you become instantly uncomfortable. The problem is that the discomfort you feel is quickly interpreted as a threat. When your brain senses a threat it makes a quick suggestion: get into fighting stance.

In other words, you are going to do the battle with the normal and natural reactions in your own mind. You *must* guard against this reaction. Nobody wins when you meet their meanness with your meanness. That doesn't mean you are required to stand there politely if someone is lobbing f-bombs at you, or worse, making threats. But you cannot allow their negative attitude to take you off your positive energy mindset.

As the salesperson, you need a proper perspective on this dynamic. You need to understand that your customer is going through a difficult time in a highly emotional decision-making process.

The Rationale Behind the Meanness

The fact is, your customer is facing an abnormal situation. They are making a major purchase decision. We would do well to learn from psychologist Viktor Frankl who once said, "Abnormal behavior in abnormal situations *is normal.*"

If you think about it, you are not any different. Wouldn't you admit that you are a better person at a cocktail party or a wedding reception than you are when you walk into a car dealership? Most of us are.

Seek First to Understand

You sell your product every day. How often does your customer buy what you sell? In all likelihood, it's just not that often. That puts your customer in uncharted territory.

In making a major purchase decision your customer is facing a situation that is not normal to their everyday experiences.

But if you stop and consider that the *environment* is triggering the negative energy, it changes everything. As I said previously, at this point we see behavior, not character.

Just as you would have empathy, compassion, understanding, and—above all—patience when a customer is going through a trying time, can you not look at this buyer the same way?

Outlast to Win the Battle

The battle is over energy, the customer's negative energy vs. your positive energy. This is a battle that you cannot afford to lose.

Make the unilateral commitment to outlast this customer. When you make the decision to display positive energy before that customer even walks through the door, you are committing to something that is independent of the energy the customer displays.

YOU make that decision, and therefore only YOU can decide to move from positive to negative energy. Don't do it. Stay positive until that customer comes around.

The Good News

This customer is likely to visit your competitors. That means that he or she is likely to display the same negative energy. There is a strong chance that this prospect will be treated poorly and cast off in other sales environments by salespeople who are weaker minded.

That's great news! It means that this customer is yours for the taking…if you are willing to be patient enough to outlast their negative energy.

Summary

When you outlast the negative prospect, it's amazing what can happen. Remember, someone during the conversation is going to change. Be determined to bring the customer up to your positive frame of mind. If you do, everyone wins!

SELF-STUDY QUESTIONS:

1. *Think of a recent prospect or buyer you worked with who fits the characteristics of a "mean customer." How did you handle your interactions with them? What would or could you have done differently to make the interaction with them more positive and productive for you and them?*

2. *What can you do when you start your day to ensure you are maintaining a positive perspective and attitude throughout the day? (e.g. come up with a mantra to repeat, post a checklist of quick actions to take before interacting with a customer, etc.)*

3. *What do you think are the characteristics of a positive person?*

Dealing with Challenging Customers In Sales
Confused Customers

CHAPTER 3:

Confused Customers

Insurance Agent: *"Okay, you're all set on your auto insurance. Do you want to discuss an umbrella insurance program?"*

Insurance Shopper: *"I live in San Diego. I don't even own an umbrella."*

You know that one customer who simply doesn't "get it"? You explain three different times in three different ways, but in the end you just get a blank stare.

This often happens during the sales conversation when you present a technical concept that the customer just can't seem to grasp. You ask a clarifying question to make sure they comprehend only to hear a response that is completely out of left field. They simply cannot connect the mental dots.

Your patience grows thin, the customer's frustration goes up, and in the end the prospect walks away. And why? Because of a critically important principle that you must understand:

A confused mind says "No!"

That's right. A confused mind simply cannot move forward with a purchase decision. There is too much cognitive strain to deal with, and that tension causes the brain to go into default mode. The default is to stay with what they have.

The Frustrated Sales Professional

This situation can be extremely vexing to the sales professional. You're just trying to be helpful. You explain things every which way. I admit—it can be frustrating.

If you are not careful, you might brand the customer as being dim-witted in some way. You say to yourself, "Well, I guess this guy just isn't that smart."

Of course, nothing good happens when you resort to detrimental judgments about your own prospects.

How Are You Smart?

Noted British educationalist Sir Ken Robinson poses a very interesting way to assess the brainpower of individuals. We have been taught to assess the mental capabilities of people by asking the question, "How smart are you?" We gauge this assessment by evaluating test results.

Robinson says that this is the wrong question. Instead, we should be asking, "How are you smart?"

Sir Ken Robinson's point is that people are smart in different ways. Some are more technically intelligent. Others more socially intelligent. And others more creatively intelligent.

When we think about the trait of intelligence, we may think that people who are more linear in their thinking are more intelligent. That's not necessarily the case. Some people think in pictures. Others in numbers. And others in emotions.

Your customer is not stupid just because they are confused about your product. It might simply mean that they have a different learning style (or different experiences or a different background from yours) that requires a different approach from you.

Easy = Right

At Shore Consulting we have been teaching this important principle for years. "Easy equals right" is an important mental shortcut that we all use when making decisions. Your customer does precisely that.

The role of the sales professional is to take a complex product or process and explain it in a simple manner.

Solving your customer's dilemma doesn't involve pounding your way through your presentation. The solution lies in breaking things down and making them simple.

For example, suppose you are selling financial services and you need to explain the tax ramifications of a particular financial instrument. You can read what you found in the fine print on the prospectus, but you will likely lose your customer in the process. Take some time to rephrase the concept. Use plain English and avoid financial-speak.

Complex = Wrong

If easy equals right, the converse is also true. *Complex* equals wrong. When a concept is too complex to grasp (when it is explained in technical terms to a non-technical person, for example), our brain defaults to rejection mode. It is a safety mechanism that switches on without conscious decision.

What do your customers sometimes find confusing? What principles, features, processes, or policies are difficult to grasp? You would do well to rethink your approach.

Simplify. Simplify.

One of the easiest ways to present an otherwise complicated concept is to utilize a story or an analogy. Use phrases like "It's like this…" or "Think about it this way. Have you ever…?"

Going back to our financial services example, suppose you are suggesting annuities to your client. You could define an annuity as follows: "Annuities are legal and financial indentures between individual investors and large insurance conglomerates, whereby investors agree to pay an allocated amount of premium and at the termination of a pre-determined fixed term, the insurer will guarantee a succession of disbursements to the insured party."

You would probably be better off with a brief flyover of the definition first: "When you retire you need to replace your lost income. With an annuity, you are investing a big chunk up front and then you are receiving small payments for a long period of time. It's a good way to add consistent income when you need it most."

If your customer can place themselves into a story it is so much easier for them to understand the concept.

Summary

Everybody learns differently. Everybody has a different background. Be patient with the person who has a different learning style than yours or has not experienced the same things in life that you have. Be empathetic with them. Give them the message in the way they need to hear it.

Remember…easy equals right. And when it's right, it's easier to make a sale.

SELF-STUDY QUESTIONS:

1. *Think of a recent prospect or buyer you worked with who fits the characteristics of a "confused customer." How did you handle your interactions with them? What would or could you have done differently to make the interactions with them more pleasant and productive for you and them?*

2. *What do your customers sometimes find confusing? Identify a principle, feature, process, or policy that is the most difficult for your customers to grasp and write out a simple explanation for it.*

3. *What can you do to ensure you remain calm and patient with confused customers?*

Dealing with Challenging Customers In Sales

Greedy Customers

CHAPTER 4:

Greedy Customers

My guess is you've heard this one: "I'm sure you've got a little more room in this deal. I won't pay any more than I have to!"

Let's take a look at the greedy customer, that individual who is not going to settle for anything less than the best terms they can get. I'll be honest with you–they can be tough. But if you look beyond—actually behind—the behavior, it will make the sales process much more manageable.

The Scenario

So here you are, working with a customer who is constantly asking for more. More of what? Well, everything basically. They want a better deal. They want better terms. They want more add-ons. They just keep working you and working you and working you, attempting to talk you down on your price or up on your discounts.

If you are not careful your mind will want to default to a perspective that makes you feel better in the short run but causes great damage over time. You will begin to make moral judgments. You will begin to label. You begin with the "justs."

"He's just greedy." "She is just stingy." "He just wants more money." "She is just irrational."

The Paradigm

As in the previous chapters, I want to start by looking at the mindset involved. In this case I want to consider two mindsets—theirs and yours.

Consider this. Your so-labeled greedy customer may very well have been raised in a household (or a culture) where asking for things is commonplace. In their background, it may be normal to ask… and ask…and ask again. Your customer may simply have a different paradigm—a different way of thinking—when it comes to the sales process.

For example, what happens when you go to the store to buy a loaf of bread? You go to the shelf, you look at the loaf of bread, you look at the price tag, you decide to buy it, you pick it up, you go to the check-out stand, you give the clerk a couple of bucks and you walk away. That's your purchasing paradigm.

But for many cultures, you lose the buyer with the very concept of a price tag. Price tag? What's a price tag? In their minds, there is no price tag. You pick up the loaf of bread and you proceed to negotiate with the clerk in order to get the best price possible. That is their purchasing paradigm. That is their perspective. That is what they know.

Perhaps it is not a cultural difference, but simply a matter of modeling from their parents or their nurturing environment. The old man taught you that virtually everything in the world is negotiable.

When this greedy customer comes into your sales environment with their completely different purchase paradigm they will interact with you in a very different way. It does not make them wrong. It does not make them rude. It does not make them aggressive. It just makes them…them.

The Value of a Dollar

I would take it even one step further. Many customers are very hard-driving when it comes to negotiations and requests. They work you over relentlessly in search of one more dollar to be included in the deal.

Does that make them greedy? Not at all. It might only mean that they value that one dollar more than you do. They work hard to earn that one dollar, and because they work so hard they deeply appreciate the value of that dollar. It is simply not honorable to leave that dollar on the table. And the only way to ensure the best terms is by asking and asking and asking again.

It's not about their character; it's about their style. That's a big difference.

Firm and Final

When you find yourself in a situation with a buyer who wants everything, I suggest you remain calm but firm. Say something like this:

"You have found my last price. This is it. The price does not get any better than it is right now. So, if you ask me for another 1% off are you going to walk away? I don't want that to happen, but I'm going to let you walk away. Because this is our last price."

That is what your customer needs to hear. They need to know that this is the final price, that it's fair and that you are not going any further. When they believe that the price is fair and final, you've reached that wonderful place called value purity.

Summary

Get your mindset right first. Practice your firm but fair description of the "last price." Then stick to your guns. Remember, this customer isn't trying to be mean. And they are not trying to take advantage of you. They are just being who they are.

So, let them be who they are. Work with them to try and close the deal. Sure, they will make you work for it. But in the end, it will be well worth it.

SELF-STUDY QUESTIONS:

1. *Think of a recent prospect or buyer you worked with who fits the characteristics of a "greedy customer." How did you handle your interactions with them? What would or could have you done differently to make the interactions with them more pleasant and productive for you and them?*

2. *What specific steps can you take to practice working on your responses to greedy customers?*

3. *What do you think is the best response to a greedy customer? Write out a script you can use to practice remaining calm and firm with a greedy customer.*

Dealing with Challenging Customers In Sales

Unreliable Customers

CHAPTER 5:

Unreliable Customers

Your product: Second homes in a resort area.
Your buyer: Well-off but not exactly rich.
The process: Strategize on how to get a lender to say yes to a sizable loan.
The problem: Your buyer is a flake.

Or is she?

In the partnership between a salesperson and a customer, you'd like to believe you are going to have a responsive, supportive, cooperative buying partner. She will make the purchase her personal priority, she will walk with you step-by-step throughout the process. She'll even write a glowing review at the end.

Alas, what we want and what we get are often vastly different.

Stay in the sales business long enough and you are bound to run across customers who are not particularly reliable. Sometimes they are a little flaky. Sometimes they are a little elusive. You think they are going down the path with you…but without warning they fall off the radar. You can't nail them down. They are slow to return your calls. What is up with that?

I would suggest there could be a lot of things "up with that." But once again, as has been a consistent theme throughout this series, you may simply be dealing with a style difference.

That second-home buyer might be the world's biggest flake. Or she might just be really, really busy.

True Confession

You may not like what I am about to say, but here it goes: *I'm that guy.*

I am the type of buyer who can drive a salesperson a bit crazy. I tend to start off excited about purchasing and I can be extremely cooperative early on.

But then something happens. And what is that something? It's life.

Many of your customers live exceedingly busy and largely unstructured lives. Reality for them is go, go, go. They tend to overcommit. They have a thousand responsibilities. They are always behind. And they are difficult to pin down.

That doesn't make them bad people. They may appear to be unreliable, but really their lives are just hectic or even chaotic.

I'm not here to make a moral judgment on that behavior. I'm just letting you know that there are people out there who are busy, who are distracted, maybe even have a little attention deficit. Some may be seriously plagued with the "squirrel syndrome."

My Client Maggie

I have a large client headed by a CEO named Maggie who doesn't know the meaning of slow. I've never met anyone in my life who can keep more balls in the air at the same time. She is a human cyclone, spinning through life at breakneck speed.

Consequently, it's a roll of the dice whether Maggie will return a call or an e-mail. If I need something in a hurry, Maggie is probably not the person to talk to. At any given moment she is deciding what she should and can pay attention to.

Paying attention. I chose those words carefully, and you should, too. Think of attention like a currency. Your customer has only so much attention currency at any given time, and she must decide where to spend it, where to "pay attention."

The strategy with Maggie is simple in concept; you need to make sure you are worth her valuable and limited attention.

Being Attention-Worthy

I want to suggest that this is the type of person who needs you the most. This is an individual who needs you to partner with them despite their business and supposed flakiness, to be a personal guide through their sales journey.

I want to suggest a key statement that you can and should use at the very beginning of the partnership with your customer: "Tell me how I can make your life easier."

For this type of buyer, that is what they need more than anything else. They need to know how their life can be easier.

For the Maggies of the world, life is already far too complicated. What would it mean to have someone dedicated to making life easier?

Taking this approach early on will separate you from every other sales professional. Then you just need to stay with them, and stay with them, and stay with them. They will be all over the map. They will dart about here and there. They will get sidetracked by shiny objects. But if you stick with them, you'll earn a significant competitive advantage.

That elusive buyer, that unreliable customer, still needs to buy, just like everybody else. If you hang in there with them and do everything you possibly can to make their life easier, you will have the best strategy for creating a successful sales conversation and achieving a final purchase.

So, if you've got an unreliable customer, make that extra call. Take advantage of each face-to-face visit. Go the extra mile. Your customer will appreciate it and, in the end, their lives will be what they wanted from the start: easier.

SELF-STUDY QUESTIONS:

1. *Think of a recent prospect or buyer you worked with that fits the characteristics of an "unreliable customer." How did you handle your interactions with them? What would or could have you done differently to make the interaction with them more pleasant and productive for you and them?*

2. *What specific things could you change in your sales presentation or process to make an unreliable customer's buying experience easier for them?*

3. *What do you think would be the best approach to follow up with an unreliable customer?*

. . . .

. . . .

. . . .

. . . .

. . . .

. . . .

. . . .

. . . .

. . . .

. . . .

. . . .

. . . .

. . . .

. . . .

. . . .

. . . .

. . . .

. . . .

Dealing with Challenging Customers In Sales

Emotional Customers

CHAPTER 6

CHAPTER 6:

Emotional Customers

Salesperson: *"What do you think?"*

Customer: (Gasps) *"It's only everything I've ever wanted in my entire lifetime! OMG – it's absolutely perfect! BUT – what if I can't afford it? What if I fall in love only to have this beautiful object ripped from my very hands? Could my heart ever endure?"* (Begins to sob)

Salesperson: *"Umm…it's just a toaster."*

We like to think that all of our customers will be even-keeled and perfectly balanced emotionally. We would also like to think that we're all bazillionaires and have our own yachts moored on our own private islands. But that's not usually the way it works out in real life, is it?

Here's the deal: You are always going to have those customers who are more emotional than others during the purchase process. They are susceptible to the highs and lows of life. They can be unpredictable. They definitely go through their share of Kleenex.

Here's the dilemma for salespeople: If we match these prospects emotion for emotion we will feed emotive fuel to the emotional fire. But if we take a clinical and analytical approach we risk alienating this customer altogether.

The Plus Side of Emotion

We tend to look at the emotional levels of a prospect as if the emotion is a bad thing. It's not. In fact, our purchase decisions are made on the basis of 85% emotional input, supported by 15% logical input. It is the absence of emotion that makes for the most difficult sale.

Our purchase decisions are far more non-conscious than we think they are. These decisions are made deep in our gut. The emotion makes the call; the logic answers. The gut says, "I want that!"; the logic says, "Here's a reason why you should have it."

I would wager that the most enjoyable selling situations you have ever had were with people who were emotionally involved. I would also wager that the most un-fun transactions were with people who were completely analytical without a trace of emotion.

The Strategy: Stabilizing Empathy

If you want to help your emotional customer move through the purchase process, you need to connect with them through a sense of empathy.

Rather than thinking, "How can I match this customer's emotion?" ask yourself questions like, "How can I empathize with what this customer is going through?" or "How can I support them as they move through the purchase journey?"

You don't have to feel the same level of emotion in order to have empathy for them. Your customer doesn't need you to match their emotion. They just need you to understand it.

One of the things you want to do with the highly emotional customer is to make sure you are prepared to come alongside and recap what they are saying, and more importantly, how they are feeling.

Say to that customer, "Okay. Let me pause here for just a second. I want to make sure I'm clear. It sounds like the biggest issue you are dealing with right now is this…Did I get that right?"

By taking this approach, the emotion-driven customer knows you are not only listening to them but you are understanding them, which is far more important. Only when you truly understand someone can you truly empathize with them.

Focusing Your Feelings

If you have a customer who is emotion-driven, focus your energies on understanding how they are feeling and make sure you share these thoughts with them.

Do this a lot. Do this throughout the sales process. They will greatly appreciate your efforts and respect you for it, because they know you are experiencing the process with *them*.

Here's the good news. When you connect with that emotional customer, those are the easiest sales you will ever make. That's because sales made out of emotion are quicker and more enjoyable than sales made purely out of logic.

So, go after that emotional buyer. Embrace them. Empathize with them. And enjoy the ride. If you do, I guarantee it will be one of your most gratifying sales experiences.

SELF-STUDY QUESTIONS:

1. *Think of a recent prospect or buyer you worked with that fits the characteristics of an "emotional customer." How did you handle your interactions with them? What would or could have you done differently to make the interaction with them more pleasant and productive for you and them?*

2. *What specific steps can you take to practice working with highly emotional customers?*

3. *What approach would you take to support an emotional customer throughout their purchase decision? Write out some examples of statements you could use to show empathy to an emotional customer.*

. . . .

. . . .

. . . .

. . . .

. . . .

. . . .

Dealing with Challenging Customers In Sales

Indecisive Customers

CHAPTER 7

CHAPTER 7:

Indecisive Customers

Customer: *"I'd like to get it in blue."*

Salesperson: *"Blue. You got it."*

Customer: *"Unless it comes in red."*

Salesperson: *"I can get you either. Which would you prefer?"*

Customer: *"Well, I prefer yellow."*

Salesperson: *"Why didn't you ask for that?"*

Customer: *"Because I also prefer blue. And red. And green."*

Salesperson: *"Kill me now."*

We have come to the final chapter in this book on dealing with challenging customers. And as I bring things to a close we are going to consider our last tough buyer, the indecisive customer. You know, that person you believe is interested, that you think has found what they are looking for, but that you can't seem to get over the finish line. You can't get them to commit.

I'm going to suggest this is a particularly difficult problem for one important reason: The longer a prospect stays in the buying cycle without making a decision, the less likely it is they will make any decision at all. Make no mistake—long buying cycles are never good.

Why is this the case? Because the longer a customer stays in the buying cycle without making a decision, the further removed they get from their initial emotional impulse. Our customers, like us, are emotional beings. We make purchase decisions primarily from our gut and then we support these decisions with logic. When a prospect stays in the process for too long without making a decision, they become unmoored from their initial emotional impulse. They rely on logic and analysis alone, which is contrary to the way they really want to purchase.

Bottom line: The longer they stay indecisive the harder it is to pull the trigger.

A Case Study

It's summertime and a neighbor invites you out for a day on the lake. You don your swimsuit and put together a picnic, and you proceed to have a perfect day on the water.

The experience gets your mind spinning and you think, *"If I had my own boat I could do this all the time. How fun would that be?"*

You visit a boat store and find that the new boat you really want will set you back $30,000. That's far more than you wanted to spend, so you tell the salesperson you want to think about it.

From there you become the king (or queen) of Google. You visit every manufacturer's website you can find. You hang out on boat-lovers' forums. You read reviews. You read opinions and data points that are so diverse as to be mind-boggling.

Meanwhile, the initial salesperson you spoke with is asking for a commitment, but you are so overwhelmed with information that you simply cannot decide. You are the indecisive buyer.

And what do you need more than anything else? Someone to press the issue.

The Solution

How do you deal with the indecisive buyer? It's a two-step process.

First, you assure your prospect that they have all the information they need; adding more facts and analysis will only confuse the issue further.

Second, you ask for a decision.

It sounds like this:

> *"I want to suggest that you already have all the information you need in order to make a wise decision. Might I suggest that the easiest way to do this is to just make the call. This is the boat that works best for you, right? Just make the call: Would you like to purchase it today?"*

You might say that the approach is abrupt, and I would tend to agree with you. But that question takes customers out of contemplation mode and puts them in decision mode.

The rule of thumb with indecisive buyers: Ask a closing question. Cut off the mental gyrations and get them into yes-or-no mode. You'll be doing them a favor.

You might be hesitant to take this approach by thinking, "If I ask them to buy, I might put them off." I would suggest that If you ask them to buy, you are going to force them to contemplate a decision. I'm not saying to be pushy or manipulative. This approach is not for you. This is for them.

The earlier we ask them to consider purchasing, the more we are helping them go through the deliberation process while their emotions still weigh in on their decision.

When we rob people of an emotional interest in a decision, they make bad decisions. We are built to make decisions based on emotion and supported logic.

When you start seeing the hemming and hawing, you need to immediately set the table to ask the closing question, to ask the customer to make a purchase decision.

When you do that, you keep the customer's emotion in the mix. And this is a good thing. When a holistic purchase decision has been made, the buyer is happy. You are happy. And it makes the purchase experience much more enjoyable for everyone involved. In sales, it doesn't get any better than that.

SELF-STUDY QUESTIONS:

1. *Think of a recent prospect or buyer you worked with that fits the characteristics of an "indecisive customer." How did you handle your interactions with them? What would or could have you done differently to make the interactions with them more pleasant and productive for you and them?*

2. *What specific steps can you take to practice working on your responses to indecisive customers?*

3. *How would you ask an indecisive customer to make the purchase? Write out a closing script you can use to practice asking an indecisive customer to buy.*

Don't Let Your Team Settle For "Good Enough"!

ORDER A BUNDLE OF 10 AND SAVE

Handling Sales Objections

The Keys to Unstoppable
Sales Success

FREE BONUS GIFT:
Order now and you'll receive an instant bonus:
JEFF'S SALES TRAINING VIDEO SERIES

visit jeffshore.com